Peace in the Classroom

Peace in the Classroom

Practical Lessons in Living for Elementary-Age Children

Hetty Adams

PEGUIS PUBLISHERS
WINNIPEG • CANADA

Printed and bound in Canada by Hignell Printing Limited

95   96   97   98   5   4   3   2

Canadian Cataloguing in Publication Data

Adams, Hetty, 1949–

    Peace in the classroom

    ISBN 1-895411-68-8

1. Classroom management. 2. Classroom environment.
3. Education, Elementary – Activity programs.
LB3013.A33   1994   371.1'024   C94-920193-6

Book and Cover Design: Laura Ayers

Peguis Publishers Limited
100–318 McDermot Avenue
Winnipeg, Manitoba
Canada R3A 0A2

toll free 1-800-667-9673

In memory of Ben, who continues to inspire me; and for Joe,
who encourages me to preserve hope.

Contents

Preface

One day, when my son Ben was five, he and I were enjoying the late afternoon sun on the beach. Although engrossed in my book, I had noticed another young boy playing nearby. I was surprised, therefore, when Ben sat down beside me looking upset. I asked him what was wrong. "That boy needs some 'Lessons in Living,'" he replied. As I looked up, the other boy was in the final stages of destroying the sand castle Ben had spent the afternoon building.

Ben was attending Unity Elementary School in Delray, Florida at that time. An important part of the school curriculum was "Lessons in Living," described in the school handbook as "lessons to enlighten young people to believe in themselves, to believe that they are important and can be a powerful influence for bringing about needed changes for good in our society and in our world."

Ben took these lessons seriously. He was a kind, peace-loving child who treated others with respect. Ben died two years ago at the age of fourteen. He was in ninth grade and had been attending school in Halifax, Nova Scotia, after our move back to Canada.

My reflections on Ben's life always include fond memories of his early schooling, which was based on a philosophy that taught compassion, fairness, cooperation, and respect for all living things.

In my own teaching career of more than twenty years, I have worked in many schools, from a one-room school in a Newfoundland outport to a residential school for the blind in Montreal. In every one of these schools specific time allocations ensured a reasonable balance existed among all subject areas. Percentages of time were given to language arts, math, science, social studies, health, and so on. In none was time allocated for education in human values.

As teachers we do a good job educating our students in all the essential academic skills. Our students are capable and confident readers and writers, can discuss global issues, and can solve problems in math and science. Yet, we neglect to teach them the most important skill of all—how to live in harmony with one another.

This book is for the ever-growing number of teachers who have made the decision to create a more peaceful classroom environment—a place where children are learning to deal positively with the world in which they live.

Our children are the peacemakers of the future. It is up to us to equip them with the "Lessons in Living" they will need to develop a personal sense of responsibility in society.

Acknowledgments

My special thanks goes to Julie Coolen for her role in making this book a reality. I would also like to thank the following people: Judith Carter, Danielle Hessian, Connie Jacobs, Karin Myers, Glynnis Ross, Michelle St. James, and especially my family for their motivation and encouragement.

Thanks, too, to Frank MacCormick for believing in me; the teachers of Bedford Junior Elementary School for sharing their ideas; my students for proving to me that "Lessons in Living" can make a difference; and finally, Brian and Joe, without whose support I could not have written this book.

Introduction

Incidents of violence are increasing in our schools (and in society at large). More often than not, the same students are involved time and time again. The consequences are frightening: in the United States, an estimated 135,000 students carry a gun to school; in Canada, a 1991 survey shows one teenager in five has had a frightening clash with a gang. In response, parents and educators have started searching for solutions to the problems we face daily in our schools.

Many school districts are now undertaking initiatives in discipline. In Nova Scotia, for example, discipline policies are being developed in response to a directive from the Minister of Education. Many of these policies, however, are no more than a list of misbehaviors and consequences. Although we can see that something about our punishment system is not working, we continue to deal with problems reactively—time that would be better spent on proactive endeavors. As one student commented after a class discussion of the new Discipline Handbook for Nova Scotia Schools, "Teachers already know how to give detentions and suspensions. We'll have to try to do better than this."

Dr. Haim Ginott says, "The essence of discipline is finding effective alternatives to punishment."[1] The most effective "alternative" that comes to mind is providing our children with the tools they will

---

1. Dr. Haim G. Ginott. *Teacher and Child: A Book for Parents and Teachers.*
New York: Macmillan, 1972: 119.

need for living in harmony with one another. Taking a proactive approach is the first step in the direction of change. The next step is finding ways to incorporate peacemaking skills into daily classroom activities.

Most teachers deal with some form of student conflict daily—conflict that usually arises from misunderstanding, intolerance, or verbal or physical aggression. Teaching our students how to deal with conflict should be a component of an overall program of peace education. Establishing a mediation program without the other components in place is not enough, however. We need to teach our children that the basis for a peaceful school is an environment in which we value acceptance of others, cooperation, positive expression of emotions, and creative conflict resolution.

How to Use This Book

Peace in the Classroom is divided into six units. Each unit focuses on a specific component of a peace education program. For example, unit 3 consists of activities that teach children good communications skills, while the activities in unit 4 encourage children to express their emotions. Each activity has an objective, materials you'll need, instructions, and questions you can use to lead classroom discussion. Some activities also include extensions; use these with older children or with those who want more of a challange.

Take a look at all the activities before you decide where you want to start. Some activities build upon a previously introduced concept, but most will stand on their own. The needs of your students should determine where you will focus your attention first. Read through each activity in its entirety before beginning; you will find the "For Discussion" questions often become a part of the initial explanations.

You can use the activities in a variety of ways. Since our philosophy of education reflects an integrated approach to learning, you might want to incorporate many of the activities into already existing curriculum areas. For example, listening is one of the language arts strands in the elementary grades. Several of the ideas in unit 3 specifically promote the development of effective listening skills.

Other ideas, such as conflict resolution strategies, can be introduced when opportunities present themselves. Another approach might be to introduce some concepts when the children are assembled together as a group—an opportunity for a "mini-lesson." In higher grades, working with partners can also be rewarding for all involved.

Because I am not a great believer in patterns and predesigned worksheets, most of the ideas are open-ended. Children are far better able to express themselves creatively when they are not restricted by such boundaries. Having tried many of these activities with my own primary students, I know that even young children will live up to the expectations we place on them. Don't be afraid to try!

We Are the Same; We Are Different

Establishing an environment in which children recognize and appreciate their commonalities, yet respect individual differences, is one of the first steps in creating a peaceful school climate.

Children come to school with a wide variety of cultural, religious, economic, and physical differences. Developing an awareness of cultural diversity is a popular current theme in many schools. To promote understanding and acceptance of cultural differences, for example, we organize multicultural festivals, featuring the food, dress, and customs of foreign countries. Yet, within our own classrooms, we often witness intolerance and see children who dress differently or who come from a different religious or socioeconomic background being ostracized.

The activities in this unit will help students build an appreciation of both self and others. When children have a healthy self-concept, they are more likely to be tolerant of others. However, this is only a

We must approach the job of creating a peaceful world with the discipline and patience of a fine gardener. We make our plans, we break the ground and prepare it to receive our seeds. We work with the cycles of growth and weather. At times we work hard, sweating in teams; at other times we quietly repair our tools in solitude. Some of our crops are fast growing and nourish us sooner than others will. The flowers give us beauty and joy throughout the season. We do a little every day, and we know that after a long period of tending and growth, a lovely harvest is coming.

—*Mary Hayes-Grieco*

beginning. Developing a spirit of tolerance and acceptance has to be an ongoing and daily process, infused into every aspect of classroom life.

By making tolerance and acceptance of diversity one of our goals, we have to allow children to express themselves creatively, in a risk-free environment. If we, as teachers, seek comfort in conformity, then our words, promoting the value of human diversity, will have little impact on our students. In the following activities, you will find children of all ages rise to the challenge of working without patterns or stencils. Each time you give children blank paper and allow them to express their ideas without fear of failure, you will be delighted by the results—a true expression of the uniqueness of each individual.

U N I T 1

Flower Garden

GRADE LEVEL: K–6

Objective

To demonstrate that differences among people make the world a more interesting place

---

You Will Need

- a variety of colored construction paper (approximately one sheet per child)
- four large pieces of heavy paper
- scissors, glue (enough for four groups)

Directions

Divide the class into four groups. Give two groups a selection of colored construction paper. Give two groups sheets of construction paper, all one color. (Tell them crayons, markers, and so on are not allowed.) Have each group make a flower garden, using only the paper it has been given. When the flowers have been cut out, have the children glue them onto the heavy paper.

When the groups are finished, display the gardens for all to see.

For Discussion

- ◆ Which garden(s) do you like best? Why?
- ◆ Look around the room. Do you see anyone wearing the same clothing as you?
- ◆ Do you see anyone with exactly the same hair color?
- ◆ Hold your arm next to the arm of the person beside you. Are your skin shades the same?
- ◆ What would the world be like if everyone looked the same?

U N I T 1

We Are Individuals; We All Fit In

GRADE LEVEL: K–6

Objective

To show that although each of us is an individual, we all belong to the human "family"

You Will Need

◆ a large, sturdy piece of cardboard (light in color)
◆ heavy-duty scissors
◆ pencils, crayons, or markers
◆ masking tape or Scotch tape

Directions

Cut the cardboard into jigsaw puzzle pieces. (You will need as many pieces as you have students.) With a pencil, lightly draw an X at the top of each piece before cutting, so the children will know which side is the top and front. Distribute the puzzle pieces to the children and ask each to draw a self-portrait, depicting a favorite hobby, interest, activity, and so on. Have the children print their names on the front of their puzzle pieces. When the artwork is completed, have the children work cooperatively to put the puzzle together. Later, tape the pieces together on the back and hang the puzzle for display.

For Discussion

- ◆ How many different things are we all interested in?
- ◆ Is there someone else in the class who shares one of your interests?
- ◆ In what ways do we all belong together as members of the human family?

UNIT 1

No Two Alike

GRADE LEVEL: 2–6

Objective

To identify and appreciate similarities and differences among us

You Will Need

- ◆ a variety of leaves
- ◆ chart paper
- ◆ markers

Directions

Have each child bring in one or two leaves. Arrange the leaves on a table and ask the children to look at them carefully, making note of their similarities and differences. On chart paper (or the chalkboard) write *Our Leaf Collection* and below make two columns: *Same* and *Different*.

Brainstorm ways leaves are the same (need water to survive, die when picked, have a stem, and so on). Then discuss how leaves are different (some have sharp points, some have smooth edges, some are green, some are brown, and so on). Record all responses on the chart in the proper column.

Our Leaf Collection	
Same	Different
~ have stems ~ die when picked ~	~ shapes ~ colors

Ask for five or six volunteers and have them stand in front of the class. Discuss ways in which these children are the same (have hair, can smile, need food, and so on). Then talk about individual differences (for example, eye color, height).

Note: Be sensitive to children with a physical handicap or health-related problem.

For Discussion

- ◆ Are there two people in this class who are exactly the same?
- ◆ Do you think there is anyone exactly like you anywhere in the world?
- ◆ What are some advantages to everyone being different?

Extension

Using an ink stamp pad and white paper, have the children make thumb prints. Pass around a magnifying glass and ask them to compare prints. Point out that no two thumb prints are the same.

U N I T 1

Things We Do Well

GRADE LEVEL: K–4

Objective

To foster the development of self-esteem in each child by identifying one thing he or she does well

You Will Need

- ◆ paper
- ◆ pencils, markers, or crayons

Directions

Assemble the children and ask each to think of one thing that he or she does well. Start the discussion by telling the children something you do well. Allow each child to share if he or she wishes to do so. Then, have the children draw pictures of themselves doing what they do well and use these drawings as a bulletin board display.

For Discussion

- ◆ How do you feel when you're doing the thing that you do well?
- ◆ Are there things you would like to do better? How can you do this?

Extension

During circle time, ask each child to look at the person on his or her left and think of a quality he or she admires in that person. Then ask the children to think of a positive quality each possesses that could be given as a gift to the person on the right. Start by modeling the process. For example, "Andrew, I'd like to have some of your patience with younger children. Jessica, I'll give you some of my ability to be a good listener."

Variation

With a permanent marker, print each child's name on an end of a Popsicle stick. Put these sticks (name side down) in a container such as a soup can. Have each child take a stick and describe a positive quality of the child whose name he or she has selected.

UNIT 1

Me

GRADE LEVEL: 2–6

Objective

To have children describe themselves in a positive, creative way to others

You Will Need

- ◆ an overhead projector
- ◆ large sheets of white paper (two per child)
- ◆ old magazines
- ◆ dark paper for mounting silhouettes
- ◆ masking tape or Scotch tape
- ◆ pencils
- ◆ glue
- ◆ scissors

Directions

Use an overhead projector to make silhouettes of the children: Tape a piece of white paper to the wall and position the child so his or her head is in the center. Flash the projector light onto the child's head so that it casts a shadow on the paper behind it. Then, carefully outline the shadow with a pencil. Place this paper on top of the second piece of white paper and cut out two silhouettes. Mount them on darker paper. (For younger children, the outlining and cutting should be done by the teacher. Children in the upper grades can help one another outline, then cut out their own silhouettes.)

When all the silhouettes are completed, have the children look through magazines for pictures depicting favorite hobbies, food, sports, and so on. Have them cut these pictures out and glue them inside their silhouettes.

For Discussion

- ◆ Do any of the silhouettes look alike?
- ◆ Did you learn anything new about some of your classmates by looking at the pictures in their silhouettes?
- ◆ Do you have things in common with some of your classmates?

Extension

Save the extra silhouettes of the children. Each day, during circle time, choose one child and hang his or her silhouette on the chalkboard. Ask everyone else to share something he or she likes about that child. As the comments are given, record them on the inside of the silhouette. With older children, pass the silhouette around and have them record the comments themselves.

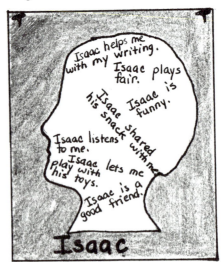

UNIT 1

Me Mobile

GRADE LEVEL: K–6

Objective

To encourage each child to develop an appreciation for his or her uniqueness

You Will Need

- clothes hangers or dowels (one per child)
- cardboard (approximately 15 cm²/6 in. sq.), five pieces per child
- scissors
- string
- markers, crayons, pencils

Directions

Pass out the cardboard to each child. Ask the children to think of four things that make them unique or special (favorite sports, hobbies and other interests, nationality, and so on). Have each child draw a different thing on each of the four pieces of cardboard. Next, have the children give the fifth piece of cardboard to a friend and have that friend draw one more thing that makes the "giver" unique. Ask the children to print a word describing each characteristic or interest on the back of each piece.

Attach the cardboard pieces to varying lengths of string and hang them from clothes hangers or dowels. Display the mobiles from the ceiling.

For Discussion

- ◆ Did anyone use the mobile to tell something about himself or herself that we did not already know?
- ◆ Why is it good to get to know your classmates well? What would our class be like if we did not know much about one another?

Extension

Have older children bring in items from home to use. Even the hanger can be replaced by something personal such as a piece of driftwood, a broken hockey stick, or a skate guard.

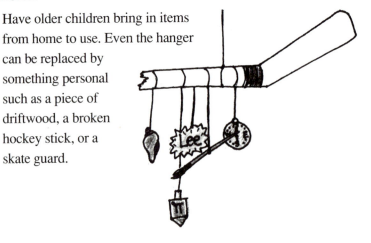

U N I T 1

We Are the Same;
We Are Different

GRADE LEVEL: K–6

Objective

To have children see that although we all have much in common, each of us is unique

You Will Need

- ◆ potatoes (one per child)
- ◆ large bag

Directions

Spread the potatoes out on a table. Give the students time to examine the potatoes and then have each child choose one. Let them spend some time with their potatoes; then return them to the bag. Collect the potatoes, then ask the children: "Do you think that all the potatoes are the same? How are they alike?" Spread the potatoes out on the table again and ask the children to find their potato. (If more than one child identifies the same potato, have them carefully look at this potato and the one left over to try to find differences.)

For Discussion

- ◆ Was it easy to find your potato among all the others?
- ◆ How did you get to know your potato?
- ◆ How is your potato unique?
- ◆ Why is it important to appreciate the unique characteristics of people?
- ◆ Explain the word *analogy,* then ask the children to draw analogies between potatoes and people.

Extensions

Use the potatoes for art projects. Some suggestions are:

1. **Potato Personalities:** Give each child a potato. Using toothpicks, have them attach carrot pieces, orange peel, spaghetti noodles, raisins, and so on, to make a potato character. Have them give their potato a name and write a story about it.

2. **Potato Printing:** Cut the potatoes in half and give a piece to each child. With sharp pencils, have them draw a design on the cut surface. Cut around each design, so it becomes elevated. Have the children dip their pattern in paint and stamp on paper.

U N I T 1

You Can't Judge a Book By Its Cover

GRADE LEVEL: K–4

Objective

To foster an awareness of the need to view differences among people without making value judgments

You Will Need

- ◆ two children's books (similar in size), one having a colorful jacket
- ◆ plain paper (enough to cover a book)
- ◆ Scotch tape

Directions

Take two children's books, each interesting and colorful on the inside. Remove the jacket from one book and replace it with plain paper, on which you have printed the title. Show both books to the children and ask which one, based on the cover, they would like to have read to them. (They will probably choose the book with the colorful jacket.) After answering the discussion questions on page 22, show the children the inside pages and ask if they would like to reconsider.

We Are the Same; We Are Different   21

For Discussion

◆ Why did you choose the book you did?

◆ Did the cover of the book tell you anything about the contents? Explain.

◆ Do you think we often judge people by how they look? Why is that not such a good idea? What should we do instead?

Extension

Have the children make books to represent themselves. On the cover, ask them to draw a picture of something everyone knows about them. On the inside, have them draw pictures of some of the things that their classmates may not know about them. For example, everyone may know that Mary is on the swim team but they may not know that she enjoys helping her dad with woodworking projects. Display the book on a bulletin board.

U N I T 1

Artifact Assignment

GRADE LEVEL: 2–6

Objective

To have children reveal some of their personal background in a novel way

You Will Need

- ◆ paper bags (one per child)

Directions

Define the word *artifact*. (Archaeologists define artifacts as human-made clues from the past that can be picked up and carried; you can define them as anything made by people.) Begin with a discussion on how history is revealed through artifacts (for example, stone tools can tell us about trade routes; pottery can sometimes tell us what people ate). Ask if anyone can think of an example of an artifact that would reveal to others something about his or her background (for example, an old photograph, a souvenir from a holiday, ballet shoes).

When the children understand the concept, give them each a plain brown paper bag and ask them to bring in ten personal artifacts from home. Give each collection a number. When the children are not in the classroom, empty the bags on to tables. Be careful to keep the contents of each bag together.

When the children return, assign everyone a number and ask them to find the collection with that number. Give the children enough time to examine the artifacts and then have them write a description of the owner, based on the contents. Do not use names at this stage. Ask each child to read the description he or she has written and invite the others to guess who the owner of the artifacts might be.

For Discussion

- ◆ Did you learn anything new about a classmate?
- ◆ Did anything surprise you?
- ◆ Did you find out that someone has more in common with you than you realized?

Extensions

Make a time capsule and fill it with current artifacts. Take a sturdy plastic container with a lid. In it, place items that are relevant to

the lives of the children; for example, an empty soft drink can, a baseball cap, a cassette of music they enjoy. When the capsule is full, seal the lid with strong tape and then bury the container in the ground.

Older children might enjoy making a permanent display/wall hanging by painting a shoe box lid black and gluing some personal artifacts inside.

U N I T 1

Friendship Fruit Salad

GRADE LEVEL: K–6

Objective

To explore the "salad bowl" concept of a multicultural country

You Will Need

- ◆ fruit (cut into bite-sized pieces)
- ◆ large bowl
- ◆ small bowls or cups, spoons (one per child)

Directions

Have each child bring in one cup of fruit, which has been cut into bite-sized pieces. Specify that any kind of fruit will do, except fruit that spoils easily after it has been cut. Mix all the fruit together in a large bowl.

Have a fruit salad feast, making a point of how wonderful it is that the variety of fruit makes such a delicious taste treat.

For Discussion

◆ Would the salad have been as good if it had been made with only one type of fruit?

◆ How is our country like a giant salad bowl?

Extension

Have the children make a graph of the favorite fruits or colors of fruit.

Reach Out and Be a Friend

Friendship is important for all children. We can help children develop positive relationships with their peers by encouraging them to get to know more about one another. In doing so, we help break down some of the boundaries that can inhibit the growth of friendship.

> Love is the most durable power in the world...Love is the only force capable of transforming an enemy into a friend.
>
> —Martin Luther King, Jr.

A classroom in which everyone shows kindness towards others is a happy place to be. Children will work cooperatively and help their peers without hesitation.

Most of the children in your class will likely spend several years together as a group. Investing time in the activities described in this unit will be time well spent for both you and your students.

Some of the ideas in this unit could be yearlong activities (for example, Helping Hands Tree, Friendship Chain). Invite the entire school to become involved. Before you know it, random acts of kindness will be the order of the day!

UNIT 2

Arms Are for Hugging

GRADE LEVEL: 1–4

Objective

To encourage children to think of creative ways to describe hugs

You Will Need

- construction paper (a variety of colors)
- lined paper
- ticketboard or manila tag (approximately 50 cm x 50 cm/ 20 in. x 20 in. per child)
- scissors
- glue
- markers or crayons

Directions

Discuss the idea that there are many kinds of hugs (for example, bear hugs, grandma hugs, puppy hugs).

Ask the children to think of other kinds of hugs and record their responses on the chalkboard. Using the following poem as a pattern, have each child write a "hug poem." (Tell older children they can expand or alter the framework.)

Hugs

Hugs, hugs,
I like hugs.

_____ hugs,

_____ hugs,

_____ hugs,

and _____ hugs.

I like hugs.

Show the children how to make a ticketboard doll. (Fold the ticketboard in half and draw the outline of a head and upper body on one side. Cut the ticketboard along the lines and the doll will be symmetrical. You may find it easier to make the head separately and attach it later.) Then, have them make their own. Add hair and facial features, using construction paper. Decorate the shirt with markers or crayons.

Have the children print their poems on lined paper and glue to the front of their dolls. Arms can fold over in a hugging position.

For Discussion

- How do you feel when a friend hugs you?
- How do you feel when you hug your friend? Next time you notice that your friend looks sad, give him or her a hug! (Remind the children that they have the right to say no if they do not want to be hugged.)

Extensions

1. Using the same doll pattern, suggest a variety of written formats or frameworks, then have the children write additional poems. For example: "I like to hug my…" (Nana, sister, teacher) and "Hugging makes me feel…" (warm, happy, safe).

2. Make teddy bear fold-outs and have the children write poems about "bear hugs."

U N I T 2

Helping Hands
GRADE LEVEL: K–2

Objective

To encourage children to think of ways in which they can
help others

You Will Need

- ◆ I Can Help Someone hand (one per child)
- ◆ chart paper
- ◆ markers

Directions

Discuss with the children ways they can help others—in class
at home, and on the playground. Stress that helping someone
involves the giving of oneself, not of material possessions. Ask
for suggestions and record their ideas on the chalkboard or on
chart paper.

Give each child an I Can Help Someone hand to complete.

For Discussion

- ◆ How do you feel when you want/need help and you are ignored?
- ◆ How do you feel when you help someone?
- ◆ How do you feel when someone helps you?
- ◆ Do you think we help others enough? Why or why not?
- ◆ Helping someone without being asked is a wonderful thing to do. Think of a way you can help one person every day. Then do it!

Extensions

1. Compile all the children's ideas on a master list. Select two ideas from each child. Have the children print each idea on a piece of paper and illustrate them. Display these on a bulletin board.

PEACE IN THE CLASSROOM

2. **Christmas Wreath:** For each child, cut out a piece of unbleached cotton (approximately 40 cm x 40 cm/16 in. x 16 in.). With pencil, lightly draw a circle (about 10 cm/4 in. in diameter) in the middle of the cotton. Have each child dip his or her palm into green tempera paint to make a handprint wreath around the outside of the circle.

When the green paint is dry, have the children decorate the wreath by dipping a finger into red paint and making holly berries. You can also glue a red ribbon to the wreath to make it complete!

Turn the top over to make a seam and glue in place. When dry, insert a piece of dowel. Attach a piece of yarn or ribbon to hang.

3. **Peace Doves:** Have the children dip their hands into white tempera paint and press onto a piece of darker paper. The

thumb becomes the head of the bird. Use a black marker to draw an eye, and orange for the beak. Cut out a small strip of green construction paper and glue it to the beak for an olive twig.

UNIT 2

New Friends

GRADE LEVEL: 2–6

Objective

To provide an opportunity for each child to become better
acquainted with a classmate

You Will Need

- ◆ chart paper
- ◆ markers, pencils
- ◆ paper

Directions

Explain to the children that they will be given an opportunity to
get to know one of their classmates better. (Although children in
a class spend a lot of time together, quite often they may go
through an entire year without really getting to know much about
some of their classmates.)

Ask each child to make a list of classmates they do not know
well. Using their lists, organize the children in pairs so everyone
has a partner. Allow the children to spend ten to fifteen minutes
each, talking about themselves to their partners. When they have
finished, ask the children to write a paragraph about their "new
friend." Invite the children to share if they wish to do so.

For Discussion

- What do you and your new friend have in common?
- Does anything you have learned about your new friend surprise you? Explain.
- Why is it important to get to know the people we work with? What would our class be like if we did not know much about each other?

Extension

Have children draw pictures of their new friends to accompany the writing. Make a class book entitled *New Friends,* using the writing and the drawings.

U N I T   2

Helping Hands Tree

GRADE LEVEL: K–6

Objective

To identify and acknowledge ways in which children help others

You Will Need

- a small bare tree or a large tree branch set in a bucket of sand
- paper
- pencils, markers
- ribbon or yarn
- colored construction paper
- scissors

Directions

Ask the children for examples of ways they have helped others in the past few days. Show them the "Helping Hands Tree," which should be in an easily accessible location in the classroom. Choose one of the children's good deeds to illustrate how the tree will be used. Ask the child to trace his or her hand on a piece of colored construction paper and cut it out. Then have the child print on the hand what he or she did, and attach a piece of ribbon or yarn to hang the hand on the tree.

Leave a supply of paper and ribbon or yarn near the tree and invite the children to add a helping hand whenever they have done a kind deed for someone else.

For Discussion

- When we start to think of our hands as "helping hands," how will that affect the way we get along with one another?
- How would our world be different if people used their hands for acts of kindness only?

Extension

Some schools have successfully carried out this theme with the entire student population. Place a large tree in the main lobby. Have a supply of paper and ribbon or yarn available in each classroom. This activity is a great way to promote school spirit!

Variation

Instead of the children recording their own "good deeds," ask them to record the acts of kindness they witness being carried out by their classmates.

U N I T 2

Helping Hands Logbook

GRADE LEVEL: 2–6

Objective

To have children identify times when they have helped others

You Will Need

- ◆ construction paper (two pieces per child)
- ◆ unlined paper (six sheets per child)
- ◆ pencils, crayons, or markers
- ◆ stapler and staples
- ◆ scissors

Directions

Begin this project on a Monday.

Have the children make their own logbooks: Tell each child to trace his or her hand on a piece of construction paper. Then, lay this on top of six blank pages and place a piece of construction paper underneath for the back cover. Staple all the pages together (at the "wrist"), and have the children cut out their books.

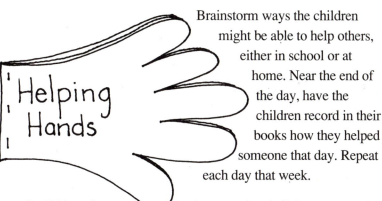

Brainstorm ways the children might be able to help others, either in school or at home. Near the end of the day, have the children record in their books how they helped someone that day. Repeat each day that week.

On Friday afternoon, having completed all five pages, ask the children to think about which deed gave them the greatest feeling of satisfaction. Ask them to record their responses on the sixth page.

For Discussion

- ◆ Was it easy for you to write something each day? Why or why not?
- ◆ Did you have several things to choose from on certain days?
- ◆ How do you feel when you help someone? Why?
- ◆ Why did you make the choice you did on the last page?
- ◆ If you had to keep a "Helping Hands Logbook" for the entire year, do you think it would be difficult to think of ways to help others? Why or why not?
- ◆ Sometimes, just listening to someone talk about a problem is helpful. Can you explain why?

Friendship Pie

GRADE LEVEL: 2–6

Objective

To develop an awareness of the qualities that build positive relationships

---

You Will Need

- chart paper
- colored construction paper (two pieces per child)
- lined paper
- pencils, crayons, or markers
- scissors
- stapler and staples
- glue

Directions

Ask each child to think about a very good friend. Invite some of the children to share their thoughts and record the qualities that are mentioned on the chalkboard or on chart paper. Once the list is fairly long, tell the children that they are going to make up a recipe for "Friendship Pie." Ask each child to decide on the five qualities that are most important to him or her, and to use these to make up a recipe. Then have the children draw a pie shape on one of the pieces of construction paper. Lay this paper on top of the

second piece of construction paper and cut out both pies at once.
Staple the pie shapes together at the top. Children can decorate
the top of the pie and glue the recipes inside.

Friendship Pie

1 cup of Kindness

1 cup of caring

2 scoops of cheerfulness

3 handfuls of sharing

½ cup of understanding

Mix together with a smile

and share with a friend.

For Discussion

- ◆ We talked today about some of the qualities you look for in others. Why did you choose these qualities?
- ◆ How do people become caring?
- ◆ Why do you think there are some people who are not kind towards others?
- ◆ Is there anything we can do if we meet someone like this?

Extension

Make a giant pie, using cardboard or heavy paper. "Slice" it and ask for volunteers to print one positive quality on each piece. (Before passing out the pieces, mark the top of each slice with an X so that when all the pieces are fitted together, the drawings are all right side up.) Have the children illustrate, then fit back together and display.

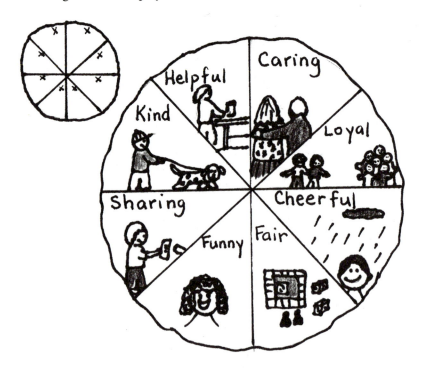

U N I T 2

Things to Do With a Friend

GRADE LEVEL: K–4

Objective

To develop the concept that friendship grows through building positive relationships

You Will Need

- ◆ chart paper
- ◆ marker

Directions

Ask the children to imagine they are with a friend on a rainy afternoon. They have no TV to watch or toys to play with. Challenge them to come up with things to do. (Discuss the idea that friendship develops when people care about each other and enjoy spending time together, and that material possessions do not have to play a part in maintaining friendships.) Write their suggestions on the chalkboard or on chart paper.

For Discussion

- ◆ Has someone ever wanted to be your friend because you had a new toy? How did that make you feel? What happened when he or she got tired of the toy?

Extensions

1. Using construction paper and crayons or markers, have each child write one of the ideas given earlier and illustrate it. Display the finished work on a bulletin board.

2. Ask the children to find pictures of children playing together. Have them cut these out and glue them onto a large cutout "smile." The smile can be made using mural paper (paper on a roll) and then hung on a wall or bulletin board.

Friendship Chain

GRADE LEVEL: K–6

Objective

To provide an opportunity for children to show kindness to people in their lives

You Will Need

- chart paper
- markers
- several paper strips (approximately 5 cm x 30 cm/2 in. x 12 in.)
- masking tape or Scotch tape

Directions

Ask the children how they can show kindness to others. Record their ideas on chart paper. Then, tell them you are going to make a "Friendship Chain," and on each link you will print one idea for expressing friendship.

First thing every morning of the next week, take down one link and read it to the children. Ask them to make an effort to carry out the idea before the end of the day. (Have the entire school participate.

Call the week "Friendship Week," and read the ideas over the public address system.)

Ideas

- Have the children introduce themselves to someone they have not met before.
- Do something to help the school caretaker.

For Discussion

- If we keep this kindness going for a longer time, what do you think might start to happen?
- Did anyone carry this activity over at home?
- What was it like to introduce yourself to someone you did not know?
- Have you made a new friendship through this project?

Extension

Another schoolwide project involves asking each child to complete the sentence "Friendship is…." on a heart-shaped piece of paper. (We did this the week of Valentine's Day.)

Provide heart-shaped backgrounds (with side tabs) cut out of red and pink construction paper. Join the hearts together and hang them around the interior perimeter of the school.

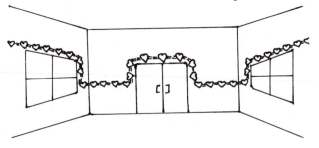

Improving Communication Skills

Much of the conflict that occurs among children arises out of communication problems. Children are usually so intent on telling their "side of the story" that they do not listen to the other person's viewpoint. An important aspect of maintaining a peaceful classroom environment, then, is acknowledging that everyone deserves the right to be heard. "Talking Stick" (page 58) is an idea that works well at all age levels. It helps focus attention on the speaker and, in a simple way, lays the groundwork for important rules of group discussion.

> Peace is people talking together with a heart in between them.
> —*Daniel (age 8)*

Children need to understand the difference between hearing and listening. Often, we find ourselves thinking about what we will say in reply, rather than really listening to what is being said. By teaching and modeling reflective listening skills, we can help children become empathetic listeners. Listening is the most direct path to understanding—and understanding is the only path to peace.

You may want to repeat some of these activities during the year. Spending time on developing effective listening skills will help your students become better able to respond to everyday conflicts that arise in school and can later be extended to the world.

Helping children become effective listeners will ultimately help them become better problem solvers.

U N I T 3

Guess Who's Talking?

GRADE LEVEL: K–6

Objective

To allow children to discover that the uniqueness of individuals is easily demonstrated by listening to their voices

You Will Need

- ◆ tape recorder
- ◆ blank cassette

Directions

While children are working, quietly go to each and record him or her speaking. To avoid identifying the speaker, ask an unspecific question (make sure you don't use names) such as, "What do you plan to do after school today?" Record their responses on tape.

When you have talked to everyone, ask them to come to the circle. Play the tape, asking the children to identify each voice.

For Discussion

◆ Were you surprised it was so easy to recognize each other's voices? Why or why not?

Extension

With older children, ask a few volunteers to record other children or adults within the school. See if the remaining children can identify these voices.

UNIT 3

Are You Listening?

GRADE LEVEL: K–6

Objective

To emphasize that confusion can occur when a listener is not able to clarify misunderstood communication

You Will Need

- ◆ a drawing (completed in advance)
- ◆ paper
- ◆ pencils

Directions

Ask for a volunteer. Allow only that student to see the drawing, then have him or her describe it slowly to the remainder of the class.

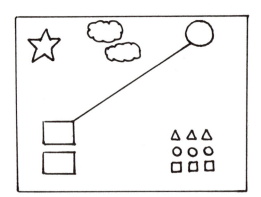

Have the children attempt to replicate the drawing from the directions they hear, without asking any questions. When everyone has finished, have the students compare their drawings to the original drawing.

For Discussion

♦ Was this more difficult than you thought it would be? What would have made it easier?

♦ Can you see that effective communication means both the speaker and listener are actively participating? Explain.

Extension

Using a different drawing, repeat this activity. However, this time, allow students to ask questions for clarification.

Compare the results with the first attempt.

U N I T 3

My Secret Friend
GRADE LEVEL: 2–6

Objectives

To have children identify a few characteristics of a classmate that make that person unique or special

To recognize individuals by listening to a brief description of their unique characteristics

You Will Need

- paper
- pen or pencil
- hat (or container)

Directions

Write everyone's name on a piece of paper. Put in a hat. Then, have each child draw someone's name out of the hat. Ask each child to think of a few characteristics that make his or her "secret friend" unique or special. Emphasize that the characteristics be positive.

Next, in turn, have each child describe the "secret friend" to the class, making sure not to use names. After each description, ask the children if they can identify who is being described.

Note: With younger children, if you volunteer to be first, you can provide a model for those children who might find this difficult.

For Discussion

- Did you have any difficulty thinking of ways to describe your "secret friend"?
- Were you surprised to hear that some of your classmates have similar characteristics to yours?
- How did it feel to hear yourself being described?

Extension

Older children can write and illustrate their descriptions for a class book.

U N I T 3

Friendly Words
GRADE LEVEL: 2–6

Objective

To develop an awareness of vocabulary that is conducive to creating a peaceful environment

You Will Need

◆ chart paper
◆ markers
◆ paper
◆ pencils, crayons

Directions

On chart paper, print the letters of the alphabet as follows:
A is for…
B is for…
C is for…, and so on.

Discuss with the children the importance of using "friendly words" in creating a peaceful classroom. Give some examples (please, thank-you, and so on).

Brainstorm an ABC of friendly words. Some letters will be more difficult than others, but children usually come up with at least one idea for every letter. Leave this chart on the wall as a

reference and a reminder to use friendly words. Following is one class's result:

An ABC of Friendly Words

A is for appreciate	**J** is for joy	**S** is for share
B is for beautiful	**K** is for kind	**T** is for trust
C is for cooperate	**L** is for like	**U** is for understanding
D is for dependable	**M** is for magnificent	**V** is for valuable
E is for "excuse me"	**N** is for nice	**W** is for wonderful
F is for friend	**O** is for OK	**X** is for eXciting
G is for gentle	**P** is for please	**Y** is for "you're welcome"
H is for helping	**Q** is for quiet	**Z** - A zillion hugs for you!
I is for interested	**R** is for respect	

For Discussion

Words can hurt as much as physical aggression. Have you ever heard the following rhyme?

> Sticks and stones may break my bones
> But names can never hurt me.

- ◆ Do you think this is true?
- ◆ When someone is unkind to you by using unfriendly language, how does that make you feel?
- ◆ How do you feel when you hear unfriendly language spoken around you?

Extensions

1. Make a class book called *Friendly Words*. Ask each child to choose a letter to print and illustrate.

2. Make a mural of pleasant things to say to a friend. (Tell students to use the ABC of friendly words for help.)

UNIT 3

I'm Listening

GRADE LEVEL: K–6

Objective

To introduce the concept of reflective listening to understand problem situations

You Will Need

- cards with "one-liners"
- puppets

Directions

Explain to the children that reflective listening means listening carefully enough that you are able to repeat in your own words what the speaker has said. It also involves listening for feelings. When we listen to someone reflectively, we show that we care about them.

Using puppets, role-play the following situations:

Situation 1

SPEAKER: I have so much homework tonight that I will never be able to finish it all.

LISTENER: It sounds like you feel frustrated because you don't think you will be able to finish it all.

Situation 2

SPEAKER: I have so much homework tonight that I will never be able to finish it all.

LISTENER: Well, if you had worked harder in class, you wouldn't have so much homework.

Ask the children to discuss how the speaker might feel about, and react to, each of these responses.

Next, pass out cards with the following "one-liners" to volunteers who feel comfortable role-playing. Ask them to find a partner who will listen reflectively and respond.

"I think the principal is going to phone my parents."
"My mother is going into the hospital."
"I don't think that's fair."
"My parents have been fighting a lot."
"I hate music class."

Some response words to use for feelings:

nervous	upset	confused
worried	angry	frustrated

For Discussion

- ◆ Did you find it easy or difficult to reflect back on what someone else said? Why?
- ◆ How do you feel when someone really listens to you?
- ◆ How do you think reflective listening can help someone work out a problem?

Extension

Ask two of the volunteers to act out their role-play. Then, discuss with the children what the next step in their conversation might be.

U N I T 3

Talking Stick

GRADE LEVEL: K–6

Objective

To provide a means of focusing attention on the speaker during group discussions

You Will Need

◆ a tree branch (approximately 40 cm/16 in. long)

Directions

Explain to the children that in aboriginal cultures it is often customary to pass a "talking stick" from person to person during council meetings. Only the person holding the stick may speak. Normally, the stick travels around the circle until all present have had an opportunity to speak.

Tell the children you would like to adapt this custom to the classroom. During group discussions, the first person to speak will hold the stick. During that time, none of the other children may raise his or her hand or interrupt in any way. Only when the speaker is finished, may others raise their hands. The speaker then passes the stick to someone else.

To practice this technique, have the children sit in a circle and ask someone to initiate a discussion on a topic of interest. Continue until everyone who wishes to has had an opportunity to participate.

For Discussion

- ◆ How was this discussion different from others that we have had?
- ◆ When it was your turn to speak, how did it feel to know that everyone was listening?

Extension

Have the children decorate the talking stick. You may want to use items that have some local symbolism. For example, in Nova Scotia, we used seashells, bits of amethyst, and an eagle feather.

U N I T 3

Communication Confusion

GRADE LEVEL: 2–6

Objective

To help children develop an awareness that confusion can occur
if the listener's attention is not focused on the speaker

You Will Need

- ◆ a copy of the story "Joe's New Bike" (page 62)

Directions

Explain to the children that you will need their help in a
demonstration. Ask for four volunteers and have them step
outside the classroom. (Be sure these children cannot hear your
explanation.) Tell the children remaining in the classroom that
the purpose of this activity is to demonstrate how difficult it is
to listen effectively when you are in a situation with many
distractions. Explain that when the first two volunteers return
to the room, they should be very quiet and listen attentively.
Then, when the next two volunteers return, they should fidget
and not listen as intently; a handful of children should then be
given specific directions such as, leave for a drink, whisper to a
friend, and so on. (Be careful not to be too obvious that this has
all been planned.)

When you are sure that the children understand what they are to do, call for the first two volunteers to return to the room. Ask one of them to read "Joe's New Bike" while the other listens and then paraphrases the story.

When they have finished, ask the other two volunteers to return to the room and give them the same instructions. After these two volunteers have completed the storytelling and paraphrasing, be sure to explain to these four children what you instructed the class to do.

For Discussion

- Ask the second pair of volunteers how they felt while they were involved in the activity. Then ask the first pair how they felt.
- Was there a difference in how well the story was paraphrased by the volunteers? Why?
- How can this demonstration help you in your daily life in school or at home?
- Can you come up with a list of good listening skills (making eye contact, listening without interrupting, and so on)?

Extension

Ask a student to design a poster, listing the listening skills that the children suggested and hang this in the classroom.

Joe's New Bike

Joe finally had enough money to buy the Cannondale Mountain Bike he had been admiring in the window of the Trail Shop for the past six weeks. It was a lot of money— $375.00—but Joe had been saving his paper-route earnings for two years.

Joe beamed with pride as he raced home, past Springvale School, where a group of his friends were playing soccer in the field.

Andrei, his best friend, hurried over to admire the new bike. He asked Joe if he could try the bike and Joe, reluctantly, said he could take it around the block.

When Andrei did not return after ten minutes, Joe began to worry. He ran to the corner where he could see Andrei, in the distance, trying to straighten out the front rim. Three other boys were gathered around. Joe raced to where Andrei was bent over the bike and started yelling at his friend, only to look up and see his beautiful new bike safely resting against a fence. Andrei grinned as he explained that he had stopped to help Craig who had fallen and damaged his bike.

UNIT 3

Recognizing Rumors

GRADE LEVEL: K–6

Objective

To demonstrate how easily stories become distorted when they are not heard firsthand

Directions

Explain to the class that this activity will help them understand how rumors often develop when stories are told and retold without verification of their truth from the originating source.

Discuss the concept of "rumors" with the children. Ask them to offer definitions and from this information come up with a collective definition that all the children understand.

Ask for six volunteers. Have four leave the room while two stay behind. Ask one to make up a brief story while the other listens, in front of the group. Then, have this child tell the same story as accurately as possible to one of the volunteers who has returned to the room. This procedure is repeated with the remaining three volunteers while the observing group listens carefully.

For Discussion

- ◆ Did you notice where the story changed from the original version?
- ◆ Why do you think that happened?
- ◆ How could this cause problems?
- ◆ What could you do when you hear a rumor about someone?

Extensions

1. Show one child a simple drawing and ask him or her to copy it from memory (number this *1*). Then have this child show his or her drawing to someone else to copy (number this *2*), and repeat this procedure until everyone in the class has had an opportunity to participate. Collect all the drawings and display them in numerical order. Be sure to include the original drawing.

2. Send a facial expression around a circle. Have the children sit in a circle so that everyone is facing someone else's back (right shoulders facing in). Ask everyone to close their eyes. Select one child to share a feeling, using a facial expression, with the person in front. Continue around the circle, having each child tap the shoulder of the person in front so that person will turn around and look. Compare the facial expression of the last child with the intent of the original feeling.

Dealing With Feelings

Humans share a wide spectrum of emotions. Some cultures encourage the open display of emotions while others find this unacceptable. In some families, boys are discouraged from showing their emotions and yet, for girls, it is considered appropriate. When children are not given the opportunity to express their feelings, eventually they will surface in one form or another. Some children may become withdrawn; others aggressive.

> We must find an alternative to violence. This eye-for-an-eye philosophy leaves everybody blind.
>
> —*Martin Luther King, Jr.*

When you encourage children to express their emotions and accept the feelings of others, you help them understand that emotions form a bond linking all humans. When we, as teachers, express our feelings of frustration or anger in a calm, rational manner, we are modeling the kind of behavior most of us hope to see in our students.

If we strive towards the goal of having children express rather than expose their emotions, we have to give them access to the vocabulary to do so. Some of the activities in this unit deal with developing the language of feelings beyond "happy," "sad," and "mad." Don't underestimate the ability of younger children to learn new words to express their emotions.

U N I T 4

Garden of Happiness
GRADE LEVEL: K–4

Objective

To make children aware that we all experience happiness but not necessarily for the same reasons

You Will Need

- light colored construction paper
- glue
- scissors
- pencils, markers, or crayons

Directions

Initiate a discussion about things that make you happy. Children usually appreciate hearing their teacher talk about personal feelings and this motivates them to share more readily.

Ask a few children to share with the others one or two things that make them happy. If the conversation moves towards "material" possessions, point out that we don't always need "things" to make us happy. Give a few examples: when I hold my baby brother and he stops crying; when I help my grandma with her garden, and so on.

Show the children how to draw flower petals, then have everyone make five. Ask the children to write one thing that makes them happy on each petal. Children can finish flowers by gluing the petals to a center on which they print, "I am happy when…"

Ask the children to make stems and leaves for their flowers. Display them with the title "Garden of Happiness."

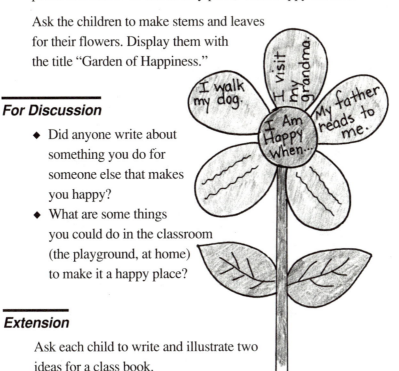

For Discussion

- ◆ Did anyone write about something you do for someone else that makes you happy?
- ◆ What are some things you could do in the classroom (the playground, at home) to make it a happy place?

Extension

Ask each child to write and illustrate two ideas for a class book.

UNIT 4

Fish for Feelings

GRADE LEVEL: 2–4

Objective

To enable children to distinguish emotions by interpreting facial expressions and body language

You Will Need

- a "fishing rod" (stick, string, and magnet)
- box
- heavy paper
- paper clips

Directions

Prior to doing this activity, make several "emotion cards": on a piece of heavy paper (approximately 5 cm x 10 cm/2 in. x 4 in.) print out an emotion (bored, frightened, happy, surprised, sad, excited, disappointed, frustrated, lonely, shocked, worried). Attach a paper clip to the card, then drop in a box.

Begin with a discussion on how sometimes we do not express our emotions verbally, but use facial expressions and/or body language. Model some feelings such as boredom, anger, or sadness. Then have a few volunteers demonstrate an emotion and have the others attempt to interpret it.

Tell the children they are going to play the game, "Fish for Feelings." Working in pairs, have one use a "fishing rod" to fish for a feeling from the box and, without showing the card to his or her partner, act out the feeling. The partner will then attempt to read the facial expression and body language to identify the feeling being portrayed.

The "fishing hole" can be set up as a center for a week or more so that all the children have more than one opportunity to participate.

For Discussion

♦ Why is it important to be able to interpret someone's facial expression or body language?

♦ How would you react if you noticed your friend looking sad? (Perhaps by approaching him or her and saying: "You look sad. Would you like to tell me about it?")

♦ When you feel angry or sad, does it help when you talk to someone about your feelings? Why or why not?

Extensions

1. Make a class book called "ABC of Feelings." Brainstorm for a "feeling word" for each letter of the alphabet and ask the children to illustrate the pages. Some suggestions:

Afraid	Happy	OK	Vain
Brave	Irritated	Proud	Worried
Curious	Jealous	Quiet	eXcited
Disappointed	Kissable	Relaxed	Yucky
Embarrassed	Loving	Silly	Zonked
Frustrated	Miserable	Tense	
Giggly	Nervous	Unhappy	

2. Supply the children with magazines and ask them to look for pictures that show various emotions. Make a class collage called "Feelings."

3. Give the children some examples of expressing happiness. Do the same for other feelings such as pride, cooperation, and so on. Have the children make a display entitled, "[*Emotion*] sounds like…" and draw speech balloons that describe that emotion.

UNIT 4

I'm Afraid; We're Afraid

GRADE LEVEL: K–6

Objective

To develop an awareness that we all have fears and should learn
to accept these feelings as well as the feelings of fear others have

You Will Need

- ◆ paper
- ◆ pencils

Directions

Introduce the discussion by telling the children one of your fears.
Ask if anyone else shares that fear. Mention some of the more
common fears people have (for example, of the dark, of deep
water, of being alone). After each example, allow time for the
children to discuss their feelings. They will soon realize that some
of their fears are felt by many of their classmates.

Working in groups of five or six, ask the children to collaborate
on a poem based on the pattern in "We're Afraid." (Mention that
rhyming is not necessary.) Each child will contribute a fear and
the group should decide on a commonly held fear for the final line.

With younger children, this could be done as a large group activity.

We're Afraid

I'm afraid at night in the dark.
I'm afraid when I hear a dog bark.
I'm afraid of thunder and lightning.
I'm afraid of getting a bee sting.
I'm afraid of some kids in the hall.
And we're all afraid of getting lost in the mall.

Extension

Tell your students: "It's OK to have fears. Let's think of some things we can do to help make these feelings go away."

◆ What can we do if we're afraid of the dark? (Turn on a night light. Leave the bedroom door open and turn a hall light on.)
◆ What can we do if we're afraid of getting lost? (Know our phone numbers and addresses.)

Discuss, in this manner, other common fears that many children seem to have.

UNIT 4

Book of Feelings

GRADE LEVEL: K–4

Objective

To recognize that all people have a variety of feelings, and to recognize and communicate how these feelings affect people in different situations

You Will Need

- ◆ blank seven-page booklets (one per child)
- ◆ chart paper
- ◆ pencils, markers, crayons

Directions

Have the children help you make a list of different feelings that people have. Write responses on the chalkboard or chart paper. Then ask them to think of a situation that makes them feel happy, sad, angry, and so on. Next, have them finish the following sentence in their books, using five feelings they can easily write about (one per page):

I feel [*emotion*] when [*action*].

Use the first page as a title page and the last page to tell about the author.

For Discussion

◆ How does it feel to be able to tell someone about your feelings? (Ask if anyone would like to share his or her book with the class.)

UNIT 4

Happy/Sad

GRADE LEVEL: K–2

Objective

To demonstrate that there are some situations in which most people react with the same emotion

You Will Need

◆ paper plates (one per child)
◆ tongue depressors
◆ markers, pencils, crayons
◆ glue

Directions

Have the children make double-sided masks. Give the children each a paper plate and on one side have them draw a happy face and on the other a sad face. Have the children glue the masks to the tongue depressors so that they will be easier to handle.

Ask the children to hold up either a happy face or a sad face as they react to the following situations:

"You are going to Disneyland tomorrow."
"Your pet cat is lost."

"You just won a poster contest."

"Your mother and father are arguing."

Ask the children for additional suggestions.

For Discussion

It is important to know that everyone has feelings and that it is good to share those feelings with others. We usually like to share happy feelings.

◆ Are there times when you keep sad feelings to yourself?

◆ Do you think that you would feel better if you shared those feelings with someone? Why?

Extension

Demonstrate how to draw a variety of emotions.

Make a class mural by inviting the children to use these facial expressions to express something that might evoke that emotion.

U N I T 4

Dealing With Angry Feelings
GRADE LEVEL: K–6

Objective

To encourage children to think of constructive ways to deal with anger

You Will Need

- ◆ chart paper
- ◆ markers

Directions

Begin by asking children to discuss the meaning of the word *angry*. Stress that anger is a natural emotion.

Ask them to share recent situations in which they felt angry and what they did about their anger. Have the children come up with a list of things people do when they are angry (for example, argue, pout, slam doors). Discuss some consequences of these behaviors.

Explain to the children the importance of calming down before reacting to feelings of anger. Ask for suggestions of ways to calm down (go for a walk, listen to music, breathe deeply, and so on). Record the children's ideas on the chalkboard or on chart paper.

For Discussion

♦ If you were angry with your parents and started yelling, how do you think they might react?

♦ If you calmed down first, do you think you would still yell at them? What do you think you might do instead?

♦ Would they react differently?

♦ How do you feel when someone yells at you in anger?

Extensions

1. Using the list of ideas for calming down, make up a song patterned on, "If You're Happy and You Know It"; for example, "If you're angry and you know it, take a walk," and so on.

2. Ask the children to make note of all the incidents of anger they see in the television shows they watch during the next week. Discuss them in class and add any new reactions to the class list "Things People Do When They Are Angry." (Remind the children that what they see on television does not always reflect reality; TV characters are not "real people.")

3. Ask each child to complete the sentence, "Next time I get angry, I will…" Have them illustrate their ideas and put them in a class book.

U N I T 4

Identify the Feeling

GRADE LEVEL: K–6

Objective

To provide children with vocabulary for expressing their emotions

You Will Need

- ◆ chart paper
- ◆ markers

Directions

Explain there are many different words to describe feelings. Offer several situations (page 80) and ask for volunteers to complete the sentences. Keep a list of "feeling words," such as the following, on chart paper.

Feeling Words

angry	sad	worried
disappointed	guilty	frustrated
discouraged	confident	lonely
embarrassed	excited	jealous
frightened	glad	surprised
hurt	grateful	elated
left out	proud	relieved

"When someone calls me a name, I feel…"

"When I have a fight with a friend, I feel…"

"When I get an invitation to a birthday party, I feel…"

"When my friends plan to go somewhere without me, I feel…"

"When I come to school without my homework done, I feel…"

"When I clean up my room without being asked, I feel…"

"When my parents have an argument, I feel…"

"When my teacher doesn't know my side, I feel…"

"When my mother promises to take me to a movie and then changes her mind, I feel…"

"When I work hard on my math problems and I can't figure out the answers, I feel…"

"When I go to a party and no one talks to me, I feel…"

"When my friend helps me with my school project, I feel…"

"When my teacher takes a long time to answer my hand, even though I'm waiting quietly, I feel…"

For Discussion

- ◆ Why is it important to be able to tell others how we feel?
- ◆ Can we express our feelings in any other way besides words?
- ◆ Is it always possible to interpret how someone is feeling by their body language? How could this be a problem?

Extension

Have the children choose one emotion from the list of "feeling words," illustrate it, and add a caption.

UNIT 4

Sticks and Stones

GRADE LEVEL: K–6

Objective

To develop an awareness that name-calling is a hurtful behavior

You Will Need

◆ chart paper
◆ markers

Directions

Print the following rhyme on chart paper:

Sticks and stones may break my bones,
But names can never hurt me.

Draw the children's attention to the rhyme and ask if it is familiar to anyone. Ask for a volunteer to explain what it means. Initiate a discussion by asking if anyone has been called a name recently. Ask that child how it felt to be a victim of name-calling.

For Discussion

- ◆ The rhyme "Sticks and Stones" was written a long time ago. Who do you think made it up and why?
- ◆ Why do you think some people call others names?
- ◆ What can you do when someone calls you a name? (Remind the children of "I" messages, page 92, if you have already done that activity.)

Extension

Invite children to rewrite the rhyme; for example:

Sticks and stones may break my bones,
But names will also hurt me.

Resolving Conflict

C onflict is a natural part of our lives. If we stop and think about the ways in which children usually handle conflict, we then have to wonder why they seem to have so few alternatives. Could it be that ignoring the situation, reacting aggressively, or appealing to a higher authority is the only reaction they have learned?

> Once the connection between conflict and violence is broken, it can be a very creative experience.
>
> —Thomas Fehsenfeld

Teaching children positive and creative responses to conflict is vital to achieving the goal of maintaining a peaceful school. The mediation process is only one technique within a framework of a unified philosophy. Conflict resolution skills can be incorporated into all aspects of daily classroom life. Skills can be introduced and reinforced as opportunities present themselves. Schools where children have been taught peacemaking skills are schools in which teachers find themselves freed from the role of disciplinarian. Children who have the ability to resolve their own conflicts are rewarded by enhanced self-esteem.

By teaching peacemaking skills, we are educating our children for the future. These skills lead to developing the kinds of thinking and behavior needed to live peacefully in a troubled world.

U N I T 5

Circle of Friends

GRADE LEVEL: K–4

Objectives

To give children a positive way of expressing a feeling of being left out

To have children develop skills to help others who have a problem

You Will Need

- ◆ sturdy paper or cardboard (enough to make one paper doll per child)
- ◆ pattern (if desired)
- ◆ scissors
- ◆ pencils, crayons, markers
- ◆ thumbtacks or pushpins

Directions

Have each child make a paper doll to resemble himself or herself. Arrange the completed dolls on a bulletin board in a circle, using thumbtacks or pushpins. (Be sure the dolls are within reach of the children.)

Explain to the children that anytime they feel left out, they can remove their dolls and place them outside the circle. When this happens, either you or a classmate will talk to the child and try to find out what initiated this feeling and attempt to help solve the problem.

For Discussion

- How does it feel to be left out of a game or activity?
- How does it feel to be included in a circle of friends?
- What are some things you can do when you are feeling left out?
- What can you do when you notice someone else being left out?
- What can we all do so that our circle of friends does not become broken?

U N I T 5

What Would You Do?

GRADE LEVEL: 2–6

Objective

To show children there are many solutions to most problems

You Will Need

- ◆ "problem cards" (pages 125–130)

Directions

Prior to this activity, photocopy the "problem cards" supplied in the appendix. Read the following problem situation to the children:

> Your dad recently accepted a job in another city and you and your family will be moving there soon. You feel upset about leaving your friends but your parents don't seem to have time to listen to your concerns.

Discuss with the children some possible solutions to this problem. Accept all responses. Once you have several ideas for solutions, point out that sometimes solving a problem is easier if you are able to talk about it with a friend.

Divide the class into groups of five or six and give each group a set of "problem cards." Ask the groups to go to a quiet area to discuss each of the problems and explore possible solutions.

Problem Card

You have a reputation for being a bully and your friends look up to you. Now you are getting tired of always being in trouble but you don't know how to get rid of your reputation.

Samples of
"problem cards"

Problem Card

You have trouble reading and some of your friends make fun of you when the teacher asks you to read aloud.

Give the children adequate time for discussion. Afterwards, go through the problems and ask for volunteers to share some of their solutions.

For Discussion

- ◆ Was it easy or difficult to come up with ideas for solutions?
- ◆ When you have a problem, do you usually talk to someone about it? Does talking to someone help you come up with new ideas for solving your problem?

UNIT 5

We Agree to Disagree

GRADE LEVEL: K–4

Objective

To identify ways of dealing with situations in which disagreement usually occurs

You Will Need

◆ chart paper

◆ markers

Directions

Discuss with the children situations when disagreement commonly occurs (for example, which TV show to watch, who starts first in a game, who gets to read a favorite book first). Ask them if they can think of a fair way to deal with these situations (flip a coin, draw straws, and so on). List their ideas on chart paper and display in the classroom as a reminder through the year.

For Discussion

◆ Did you realize solving problems could be so easy? Why don't we use these ways of solving problems more often?

◆ Will having this list in our room help you next time you have a disagreement with a classmate? Why or why not?

U N I T 5

Is Everyone Happy?

GRADE LEVEL: K–6

Objective

To encourage children to think of ways of resolving conflicts so that everyone wins (Win/Win solutions)

You Will Need

- ◆ chart paper
- ◆ markers

Directions

Describe the following conflict situation to the children:

> Ryan is practicing a song for the lip-sync contest at his school. He is excited and thinks he has a good chance of winning. Jennifer, Ryan's older sister, comes home from school and starts studying for her French exam scheduled for the next day. Jennifer can't concentrate because Ryan's music is too loud and she asks him to turn it off. Ryan is upset because the contest is the next day and he needs to practice.

At this point, ask the children if they can come up with ideas for solving this conflict so that both Ryan and Jennifer can get what they want. (Children will come up with a variety of good

---

solutions.) Explain to the children that these are Win/Win solutions.

On chart paper, lay out the following framework and ask the children to help fill in the boxes.

	Ryan	Jennifer
WIN/WIN	practices song	studies for exam
WIN/LOSE	practices song	doesn't study
LOSE/WIN	doesn't practice	studies
LOSE/LOSE	doesn't practice	doesn't study

With younger children, filling in the chart with or might be more effective.

	Ryan	Jennifer
WIN/WIN	☺	☺
WIN/LOSE	☺	☹
LOSE/WIN	☹	☺
LOSE/LOSE	☹	☹

For Discussion

- ◆ How do you think Ryan and Jennifer would feel about your Win/Win solutions?
- ◆ Why is it important that both people involved in a conflict situation feel good about the solution?
- ◆ Do you think that most conflicts can be resolved so that both people involved can be happy? Explain.

Extension

Ask the children for recent examples of conflicts they have experienced. Choose one example and, in small groups, ask the children to brainstorm Win/Win solutions. Later, ask the children to share some of their ideas.

Ask the children to come up with their own definition of Win/Win solutions. When everyone agrees, write this definition on a poster and display in the room for all to see.

U N I T 5

"I" Messages
GRADE LEVEL: K–6

Objective

To teach children a way of expressing their thoughts and feelings in a nonaggressive manner

---

You Will Need

- ◆ chart paper
- ◆ markers
- ◆ two puppets

Directions

Begin with an example of the difference between an "I" message and a "You" message. Using puppets, act out the following skits:

Skit 1: "You" Message

LAURA: I can't believe you forgot to bring in the poster. You are so forgetful! Now how are we going to do our presentation?

PETRA: Well, you wouldn't help me until last night. I was up late because of you and so I slept in this morning. I was in such a rush that I forgot the poster. It's not my fault.

Ask the children if they think Laura and Petra will be able to resolve this conflict. After a discussion, act out the second skit.

Skit 2: "I" Message

LAURA: Petra, I am very upset because we can't do our presentation without the poster. I wish there was a way we could get it before this afternoon.

PETRA: I'm sorry that I forgot it. I was in such a rush this morning. Maybe my mom can bring it over on her way to work.

Discuss the difference between these two skits. Explain that an "I" message tells how you feel without blaming or attacking the other person. When we use "I" messages, the other person realizes that we are upset, and because we are not blaming them, they are more likely to try to come up with a Win/Win solution.

A "You" message usually expresses anger and blames or criticizes the other person. People often react to "You" messages by defending themselves and finding a way to counterattack.

On chart paper, print the following "I" message formula:

Use the person's name:	_Jacklyn,_
Tell how you feel:	_I feel frustrated_
Tell why:	_when you interrupt me._
Tell what you would like:	_Please wait until I am finished._

Let the children spend some time practicing "I" messages using hypothetical situations such as the following:

◆ Someone pushes in front of you in line.
◆ A classmate has borrowed your pencil and gives it back to you broken.
◆ You are trying to read and someone keeps asking you to play.

For Discussion

◆ Do you think using "I" messages will help you resolve conflicts more easily? Why?

◆ Do you think our world would be different if everyone used "I" messages? How?

Extension

Using "I" messages is not a natural way for children to respond in conflict situations. With continual practice, however, it will become more natural and eventually be an automatic response.

Having a few additional workshops throughout the year to practice using "I" messages helps children become comfortable using them. Also, use real conflict situations as "teachable moments" to reinforce the advantages of using "I" messages.

U N I T 5

Conflict-Solving Guidelines

GRADE LEVEL: 2–6

Objective

To develop an awareness of the need to establish guidelines for conflict resolution

You Will Need

◆ chart paper
◆ markers

Directions

Ask the children how many of them play some kind of sports. Then ask if there are rules for those sports. Ask the same questions for games such as checkers, four-square, and so on. Then ask if any of the children have ever watched boxing or wrestling (organized fighting) on TV. Discuss why these sports have rules (for example, safety, fairness). Continue the discussion by asking how many of the children have rules to follow when they argue or fight.

It will soon become obvious to the children that having a set of guidelines to follow when arguing/fighting is a good idea. At this point, role-play a conflict situation with a student volunteer, who will be the victim of your anger.

The situation: A pencil is missing from your desk and you think the student took it. In this role-play, artificially escalate the conflict by name-calling, bringing up a few unrelated incidents that happened in the past, not listening to the student's story, and using anything else that seems appropriate (or inappropriate!).

Afterwards, ask the students to identify some of the things you did that made the problem worse. They will probably come up with a comprehensive list. If not, role-play the parts that they missed the first time and prompt, if necessary.

From this list, make a second list, rewording the conflict escalators in a positive way. For example, "not listening" should become "listen carefully," and so on. This second list will become your class guidelines for resolving conflicts fairly.

My grade-six class came up with this set of rules:

Fighting With Dignity

Fight the problem, not the person.
Listen with an open mind.
Use your wits, not your fists.
Don't stray from the problem of today.
Keep your cool, follow the rules.

U N I T 5

Peace Mat

GRADE LEVEL: K–4

Objective

To provide children with an opportunity to resolve conflict
without the need for teacher intervention

You Will Need

◆ a small rug or mat

Directions

Tell the children that some conflicts are easy to resolve if both
disputants are willing to look for a solution. Often, the problem is
not having an opportunity to talk things through. Explain that the
mat you have placed in a quiet corner of the classroom is a
special place where people can go to resolve conflicts. For
instance, if two children come in from lunch arguing about
something, they can go to the peace mat to try to come up with a
mutually agreeable solution to their problem. Remind the
children to use "I" messages (page 92), practice reflective
listening (see unit 3), and look for Win/Win solutions.

For Discussion

◆ Have you ever had an argument or a fight at recess or lunch? Did you resolve it? How?

◆ Have you ever felt angry all morning or afternoon because of a conflict? Did this affect your schoolwork?

Extension

Display a poster near the peace mat with the "I" message formula (page 92). With the children, make a list of listening guidelines and post it on the bulletin board.

UNIT 5

Peace Is...
GRADE LEVEL: K–6

Objective

To enable children to examine their notions of peace and come to a mutual understanding

You Will Need

◆ chart paper
◆ markers

Directions

In the center of a piece of chart paper, print the word *peace*. Ask the children to offer words or phrases that they can associate with peace. Record all responses on the chalkboard or on chart paper.

respect safe freedom
getting along
PEACE
trust
cooperation
sharing quiet

From these contributions, come up with a simple definition of peace. With older children, emphasize that peace is not necessarily the absence of conflict or fighting. Peace involves learning how to deal with conflict so that each party achieves its goal. Grade-six students made up the following definitions of peace:

Peace is when you don't need a jail.

Peace is a world where love and friendship overcome conflicts.

Peace is listening with open ears and a full heart.

Peace is being able to trust all people of the world.

For Discussion

- Do all of you wish for a peaceful world? Why?
- Do you think that most people around the world want peace?
- If everyone wishes for peace, why isn't there peace around the world?
- How do you think the world could become a more peaceful place?
- What can we do to make our school more peaceful?

Extensions

1. Invite the children to write an acrostic poem. (In an acrostic poem, a specific letter in each line, when taken in order, spells out a word, motto, and so on.) For example:

    Peace is
    Everyone sharing
    And
    Caring for
    Each other.

2. Invite each child to draw a picture of a time when he or she felt peaceful. You may have to give a few personal examples to activate their imaginations (hiking in the woods with your family, listening to a favorite piece of music, and so on). Provide circles of paper for the children to draw the scene that comes to mind and display these in the shape of the popular symbol for peace.

3. Using the heading, *A Peaceful School Is…*, invite all students to make a "brick" (rectangles of orange paper, approximately 23 cm x 10 cm/9 in. x 4 in.). Have them write their definition of what a peaceful classroom is on the brick. Next, trace the printing on each brick with a black permanent marker. Then, ask the children to do a crayon rubbing, using a real brick to give the paper a realistic look. Find an empty flat wall in your school, and attach the paper bricks to the wall.

UNIT 5

Defining Conflict

GRADE LEVEL: K–6

Objective

To enable children to examine their notions about conflict

You Will Need

- ◆ chart paper
- ◆ markers

Directions

In the center of a piece of chart paper or on the chalkboard, print the word *conflict*. Ask the children what "conflict" means to them. Record all responses on the chalkboard or on chart paper.

hitting war
unfair hate
enemies CONFLICT mean
argument bullying
fight

From their contributions, come up with a simple definition of conflict. (You may have to remind the children that a conflict does not have to involve physical aggression but can simply be opposing ideas.) Grade-six students made up the following definitions of conflict:

> Conflict is a disagreement where feelings usually get hurt.
>
> Conflict is a Win/Lose or a Lose/Lose situation that can really hurt the inside of a person.
>
> Conflict is the opposite of peace.
>
> Conflict is when people argue, disagree, or fight. Conflict can lead to war and death.

Younger children may not be familiar with the word "conflict." They will understand quite readily if you give them a playground example: "Two children are fighting over a ball. They push each other and start name-calling. These children are having a conflict." Or "The grade-two teacher and the gym teacher both want to use the gym after school. They argue and cannot come up with a solution to their problem."

For Discussion

- How many of you have been involved in some kind of a conflict recently? How did the conflict end?
- Can you think of anyone who does not experience some form of conflict at some time in his or her life?
- Does conflict always have to lead to someone getting hurt?
- Do you think you know how to handle conflict well?

U N I T 5

Conflict Cartoons

GRADE LEVEL: 2–6

Objective

To give children an opportunity to creatively share with their peers a conflict situation with a Win/Win solution

You Will Need

- ◆ cardboard box
- ◆ long strips of paper (one per child or group)
- ◆ pencils, markers, or crayons

Directions

Have the children make a "television." Cut slots (to accommodate the width of the paper strip) in the bottom and top of a box, and ask a few volunteers to decorate the "TV."

Ask the children to give some examples of recent conflict situations in which they were involved. Discuss the solutions.

Remind the children of Win/Win solutions (page 90). Show the children the TV and explain that they will be making cartoon strips of conflict situations to share with their peers. Again, emphasize coming up with a Win/Win solution.

Children can work in groups or individually. When the cartoon strips are finished, ask the children to show them on the TV. To do this, simply insert the beginning of the strip of paper through the bottom slot and slowly pull it up frame by frame through the top slot.

For Discussion

- When you watch cartoons on TV, how often do they portray conflict situations?
- Are these conflicts usually resolved? How?
- Do you think that TV cartoons help you learn peaceful ways of resolving conflict?

Extensions

1. Make a class book with the cartoon strips or display the strips on a bulletin board.

2. Ask the children to role-play their conflict cartoons.

3. Have the children collect newspaper cartoons that show conflicts being resolved. Bring these cartoons to school and display them on a bulletin board.

UNIT 5

Mediation

GRADE LEVEL: 3–6

Objective

To introduce the concept of mediation as a conflict resolution technique

Background

Conflicts are a daily occurrence in most schools and teachers seem to spend more and more time trying to resolve them. Mediation offers a new way to address an old problem.

Mediation is a process of resolving conflict with the help of a neutral third party, a mediator. The mediator acts as a facilitator and helps the disputants work out their differences cooperatively to create a Win/Win solution.

Mediation is nonjudgmental. Mediators listen carefully, without blaming or giving advice. The concept of peer mediation works because children understand and trust other children. Peer mediators do not pose a threat to their fellow students because they do not represent the "power structure" and are not in a position to impose punishment.

Directions

"The Puzzling Case" (page 110) will help children understand the mediation process. You will need four volunteers to read the parts of the children. You may want to read the part of the lunch monitor. Encourage the children to read the script a few times beforehand so they feel comfortable and confident with the roles.

For Discussion

After role-playing "The Puzzling Case," ask all students the following:

◆ What do you think might have happened if Emily and Marisa had not offered to help solve this problem?

◆ What are some things that Emily and Marisa did to help Andrew and Bianca solve their problem? Record all responses. (Your list may include: listened carefully, were fair, treated both with respect, were concerned about their feelings, asked good questions, stayed calm, and so on.) Then, from the children's responses, make up a chart entitled: *A Good Mediator Is Someone Who…*

◆ Why do you think the mediators asked Andrew and Bianca to agree to rules before starting?

◆ Do you think it was helpful to ask Andrew and Bianca about their feelings?

Extension

Following this activity, you may decide to train some of your students in the mediation process. Assuming that your students have already developed reflective listening skills through the activities in unit 3, you may decide to train some, or all.

There are three main stages to the process: introductions and ground rules, telling the story, and finding solutions. It is important to emphasize that each of these stages is vital to the process. With the framework in hand (opposite), children should be given situations to role-play, in groups of four, so they become familiar with the mediation process (monitor this role-playing carefully and add support where needed).

Mediation

Introductions and Ground Rules

- Introduce yourselves and ask the disputants if they would like help solving their problem.
- Have the disputants agree to four ground rules:
  - no interrupting
  - no name-calling or put downs
  - agree to tell the truth
  - agree to try hard to solve the problem

Telling the Story

- Ask disputant #1 to tell what happened.
- Summarize what was said.
- Ask disputant #1 how he or she feels about what happened and why.
- Summarize the feelings.
- Ask disputant #2 to tell what happened.
- Summarize what was said.
- Ask disputant #2 how he or she feels about what happened and why.
- Summarize the feelings.

Finding Solutions

- Ask disputant #1 what he or she can do to solve the problem.
- Ask disputant #2 what he or she can do to solve the problem.
- Get agreement to a solution from both disputants.
- Ask disputant #1 what he or she would do differently if this problem happened again.
- Ask disputant #2 what he or she would do differently if this problem happened again.

- Congratulate the disputants for solving their problem.

The Puzzling Case

Situation: Andrew has been working on a puzzle during the lunch hour and is almost finished. The puzzle is spread out on the floor in one corner of the classroom. Bianca has been asked by the teacher to finish a mural and needs the floor space that Andrew is using.

Bianca and Andrew are arguing when the lunch monitor walks into the room.

MONITOR: Looks like you two have a problem. Would you like help solving it?

BIANCA: Yes, please! I don't have much time to finish this mural.

ANDREW: I wish you could help. Bianca won't listen to me.

MONITOR: Well, Marisa and Emily are the mediators on duty today. Let me go get them. I think they may be able to help.

MARISA: Hello, our names are Marisa and Emily. What are your names?

ANDREW: I'm Andrew.

BIANCA: And I'm Bianca.

EMILY: Would you like us to help you try to solve your problem?

ANDREW: Yes, please.

BIANCA: Yes, and we don't have much time.

MARISA: Before we begin, we need you to agree to four rules: no interrupting, no name-calling or put downs, agree to tell the truth, agree to try hard to solve the problem. Can you both agree to these rules?

BIANCA: I can.

ANDREW: Me, too.

EMILY: Bianca, will you please tell us what happened?

BIANCA: Ms. Burchell asked me to finish this mural before the

bell rings. This is the only corner in the room without carpet so I need to work here on the floor. Andrew is only putting a puzzle together and he won't move. This mural is much more important.

EMILY: So, you're saying that you have a mural to finish before the bell rings and Andrew won't move the puzzle he is working on to let you use this floor space?

BIANCA: Right!

EMILY: How do you feel about this, Bianca?

BIANCA: Well, I feel very frustrated because I need to finish this and I am running out of time.

EMILY: You feel frustrated because you are running out of time and you have a project to finish?

BIANCA: Exactly.

MARISA: Andrew, will you please tell us what the problem is?

ANDREW: This is a very hard puzzle and I'm almost finished. I just can't pick it up and move it. Bianca expects me to destroy an hour's work. Besides, I was here first!

MARISA: So, you want to finish the puzzle you were working on and you can't move it easily.

ANDREW: Yes, and this is the only floor space that I can use, too.

MARISA: How do you feel, Andrew?

ANDREW: I feel angry because Bianca just came over here and told me to move. This puzzle has taken a long time and no one else has been able to do it.

MARISA: You feel angry because Bianca wants you to move and you would like to finish this puzzle?

ANDREW: Right!

EMILY: Bianca, what do you think you could do to solve this problem?

BIANCA: Well—I suppose I could help Andrew finish the puzzle so

that I can work here. I did that puzzle once last year anyway. It wouldn't be too hard for me.

MARISA: Andrew, what can you do to help solve this problem?

ANDREW: Maybe Bianca could help me move the puzzle. I don't think we have time to finish it. We could slide a piece of cardboard under it and move it to the table.

EMILY: Any other ideas?

BIANCA: I think moving the puzzle is a good idea. Then I still have time to finish this mural.

ANDREW: I could help you with the mural. I can at least paint in the background.

MARISA: Sounds like you two have worked out your problem.

BIANCA: Yeah, thanks for your help.

EMILY: Bianca, what would you do differently if this problem happened again?

BIANCA: Well—I shouldn't have told Andrew to move. I know that it is a hard puzzle and he was here first.

MARISA: Andrew?

ANDREW: Next time I start a puzzle, I'll work on a piece of cardboard so that I can move it easily.

EMILY: Is your problem solved?

BIANCA and ANDREW (in unison): Yes!

EMILY: Congratulations on a successful mediation. By the way, would you like us to help with the mural?

The Peaceful School

A s educators, we dedicate time and energy to creating school-wide themes of all kinds: fire prevention, nutrition, dental health, and so on. Why not develop themes around the goal of creating a peaceful school environment? What could be more rewarding? A peace theme will affect all members of the school community in a positive way.

> I wondered why somebody didn't do something for peace...Then I realized that I am somebody.
>
> —*Anonymous*

Once a school starts on a journey to a peaceful climate, there is no turning back. Peace education permeates all aspects of school life.

If your first reaction is that this is an idealistic and unattainable goal, remember that every journey begins with a single step. The first step in your journey should be a commitment by all staff members to the importance of teaching peacemaking skills. From there on the journey will be an exciting one.

Within a school community, a team spirit easily evolves when everyone is focused on the same goal. Students, teachers, parents, and administrators should be encouraged to offer suggestions for developing mutually agreed upon peace themes.

In one local school where the staff decided to focus on peace education, they came up with the following themes:

SEPTEMBER: Getting to Know You

OCTOBER: Hands Are for Helping

NOVEMBER: The Mediation Message

DECEMBER: Good Neighbors (community outreach)

JANUARY: New Beginnings (peace resolutions)

FEBRUARY: Reach Out and Be a Friend

MARCH: Together We Are Better (multicultural theme)

APRIL: Make Every Day Earth Day

MAY: We Celebrate Our Differences

JUNE: Reflections

You may want to incorporate the activities in this book with similar themes for your school.

U N I T 6

Organize a School "Peace Festival"

With a bit of planning and organization, you can hold a "Peace Festival" that involves the entire school population. Set up workshops and centers so that all the children can participate in each of the activities.

On the day of the Peace Festival, organize the children by making up small groups with cross-grade representation in each, or, by asking the children to sign up in advance for the activities and announcing time changes with the bell or a public address announcement.

The festival is an excellent time to invite guests from the community to share their common interests and expertise with the children. Parents are always happy to be involved in activities such as these and could be enlisted to help out.

Here are some ideas to get you started:

Peace Wish Pond

Use a plastic swimming pool as a wishing pond. Ask children to make a wish for peace as they throw in a coin. Donate money collected to a local charity.

Peace Quilt

Prior to this activity, precut squares of cotton (approximately 25 cm^2/9.8 in. sq.). Have children work in pairs to decorate a square with their vision of peace, using fabric crayons or markers. Solicit the help of a volunteer to sew the squares together and display the finished quilt in the school for all to enjoy.

Peace Mural

Have children write messages and draw pictures on a long piece of mural paper. If you are able to, use a bare wall in your school that needs decorating.

Paper Cranes

Read the story, *Sadako and the 1000 Paper Cranes*, by Eleanor Coerr, to the older children prior to the Peace Festival. For younger children, a simplified retelling of the story would be more appropriate. Give the children a lesson in the Japanese art of origami. Make cranes, the Japanese symbol of peace, out of paper. Display some of the cranes by hanging them from the ceiling or on bare tree branches.

An organization in Japan will send your school a certificate and a photograph of your cranes draped around their peace monument if you mail one thousand of them to the following address:

1000 Crane Club
Hiroshima International School
3-49-1 Kurakake
Asa Kita-Ku
Hiroshima 739-17
Japan

Design a Button

Give the children blank disks of heavy cardboard and ask them to design buttons. Safety pins can be taped to the back so the buttons can be worn. You may consider choosing one of the designs to have commercially made buttons produced for all involved.

Peace Doves

Papier-mâché a large punching balloon and paint it to resemble a globe. Have children make doves using white paper. Show them how to cut a slot and slip a piece of "accordian folded" paper through for wings. Ask the children to print a peaceful message on their doves. Hang the doves from strings around the globe.

Write a School Song

Have one group of students begin composing a song. Rework and refine it with each group until you have a finished song that reflects the overall spirit of the festival and the desired climate of the school. The following was written by students from Waverley Road School:

Helping Hands

(sung to the tune of "He's Got the Whole World in His Hands")

Hands are for helping, in our school.
Hands are for helping, in our school.
Hands are for helping, in our school.
Helping hands in our school.

Hands are for sharing, in our school.
Hands are for sharing, in our school.
Hands are for sharing, in our school.
Sharing hands in our school.

Hands shake in friendship, in our school.
Hands shake in friendship, in our school.
Hands shake in friendship, in our school.
Friendly hands in our school.

To involve other teachers, ask them to compose songs that the entire school body can sing during assembly. The following songs were written by Michelle, a primary teacher:

Peace and Friendship

(sung to the tune of "Twinkle, Twinkle, Little Star")

Peace and friendship in our school,
This will be our golden rule.
We can help and we can share.
Let's have kindness in the air.
Peace and friendship that's the way.
Can you make someone feel special today?

School Song

(sung to the tune of "This Old Man")

This great school, this great school,
[*name of school*] is really cool.
With sharing, caring, friendship too,
We know all the things to do.

I like you, I like you,
There is lots that we can do.
With sharing, caring, friendship too,
We know all the things to do.

Let's be friends, let's be friends,
That's a message we can send.
With sharing, caring, friendship too.
We know all the things to do.

We Love All the Children

Teach the children a different version of a favorite song;
for example:

We love all the little children,
All the children of the world.
Red and yellow, black and white,
All are precious
All are life.
We love all the little children of the world.

Discuss the meaning of the words.

Paper Dolls

Provide the children with precut dolls of different colors and give
them scraps of paper and cloth to decorate.

Conclusion

We are living in a difficult and complex world. For today's children, understanding how people relate to each other is fundamental in coping with and making sense of the world—whether it's trying to deal with a playground fight, an environmental crisis in the community, or global conflict. Given that conflict is endemic in human relationships, laying the foundation for developing positive skills in understanding and dealing with social interactions empowers our children to have a voice in the kind of world in which they wish to live.

In my classroom this year, the time I invested in "Lessons in Living" has had a positive effect on all my students and a dramatic effect on at least one. His approach to life's daily problems has changed enough that even his classmates have taken notice. Ceilidh, a grade-six student, writes:

Take an ecologically fragile planet with scarce resources and a growing population and we have a recipe for human conflict. Add conventional weapons —a recipe for holocaust. This is our challenge as a species. But we are not without resources. Add human intelligence, ingenuity, problem-solving skills. Add a deep commitment to peace, to the common good. Add the spiritual tradition of humanity. We are equal to the task. But we must prepare, educate and train ourselves to be peacemakers.

—*Northland College,*
Peace Education Studies Department

We have a subject in school called "Lessons in Living." It deals with feelings. How do you feel when someone calls you a name? It also deals with how you handle certain situations. What do you do when...? We learn to use an "I" message to express our feelings. The results of the activities are that you begin to relate better to how other people are feeling. If you think this way, there is less name-calling, less pushing at the fountain, and less discipline or punishment.

One classmate I've had for seven years has had a terrible problem with temper control and expressing himself. He's had a lot of detentions, lots of stern talking-to, but it hasn't worked. Now he's starting over with a new teacher and this subject has helped him a lot. He understands when we use "I" messages on him and can say "sorry" even if it's hard for him. He walks away from fights, which isn't easy for him. His instinct may be to fight but he tries to avoid conflict.

Nurturing a peaceful classroom takes time and commitment. The time and commitment we invest in teaching our children the skills they need to be responsible and caring individuals may well be the greatest gift we can give to them and to the world.

Appendix:
Blackline Masters

I can help

I can help

I can help

I can help

I Can Help
Someone

I can help

Your younger brother often borrows your clothing without asking and then doesn't take good care of it.

You have a reputation for being a bully and your friends look up to you. Now you are getting tired of always being in trouble but you don't know how to get rid of your reputation.

There is a girl on your street who has begun bullying you after school on your way home.

You are having trouble understanding math but you are too embarrassed to ask your teacher for help.

For the activity What Would You Do?, page 86

Problem Card

The teacher gives you a "C" on an assignment and you feel you deserve a higher mark.

Problem Card

You are with a group of friends and they start telling racist jokes that make you feel uncomfortable, but you don't know what to say.

Problem Card

You work very hard and do your best in school but your father always expects you to do better.

Problem Card

You are shopping with your best friend and she steals something.

Everyone in your class wears expensive sneakers. You are embarrassed because your parents buy old-fashioned shoes for you.

You have a friend who wants to be exactly like you. At first you were flattered but now it is starting to annoy you.

You are much taller than everyone else in your class and often get teased.

You have started in a new school and the children in your class seem to ignore you.

For the activity What Would You Do?, page 86

When you and your friends are skipping rope, the younger children keep jumping in and ruining your game.

Your teacher has invited all parents to the class fair. You feel left out because you are living with a foster family.

Some children chant and pretend to beat drums whenever Marie, a Mohawk, walks by them.

Some of the children in your class have made up a game called Chinese Fighters. This makes Sojata, who is Chinese-Canadian, feel uncomfortable.

For the activity What Would You Do?, page 86

Your parents often promise you things. When you remind them, they accuse you of being greedy.

You worry your mother will come to the class after she has been drinking.

You enjoy sports but are always the last one to be picked when teams are chosen.

Your father doesn't like your best friend and won't allow her to come to your house.

For the activity What Would You Do?, page 86

You like to draw but your parents discourage you because they think you are wasting your time.

You have trouble reading and some of your friends make fun of you when the teacher asks you to read aloud.

Your best friend asks you to do her assignment for her. You're afraid if you say no she won't talk to you anymore.

Someone in your class has said something unkind about you. When you confront him, he denies saying anything.

130   From *Peace in the Classroom* by Hetty Adams. © 1994 Peguis Publishers. This page may be photocopied for classroom use. Note: photocopy at 135% for actual size.

For the activity What Would You Do?, page 86